Contents

Introduction

This *Study Guide* is a tool to accompany the third edition of *What Great Principals Do Differently: Twenty Things That Matter Most* by Todd Whitaker. It is a practical resource for educational leaders who are examining what great principals do that sets them apart from others. This guide will provide assistance to instructors, staff developers, professors, or any other educational leaders who are working with principals to hone their leadership skills. In addition, principals reading and studying Whitaker's book can use this guide as a "workbook" for the original text. This companion guide will serve as a road map for helping principals focus on the leadership beliefs, behaviors, attitudes, and commitments that have a positive impact on teaching and learning in our classrooms and our schools.

The third edition of *What Great Principals Do Differently* is filled with practical, common-sense advice for principals serving at the K–12 levels. Whitaker's book focuses on what great principals do that sets them apart, clarifying best practices based on research and numerous school-based studies and visits. Ultimately, Whitaker's book is one that principals can read and *use*—and put to use immediately. This guide, therefore, is written in a way that allows the facilitator to exhort principals involved in the study not only to read and understand essential concepts, but also to take these concepts back into their schools and implement new strategies and ideas in a practical and relatively simple manner.

Each part of this book corresponds to one or two chapters of *What Great Principals Do Differently*. To help you plan and organize your study sessions, each chapter is divided into the following five sections:

- **Key Concepts**: These summaries of the key points for each chapter in the book will help you review and focus your thoughts.
- **Discussion Questions**: These questions and ideas help you learn more about yourself and your colleagues and will aid constructive conversation in the study group, workshop, or classroom setting.
- **Journal Prompts**: Based on the specific contents of each chapter, the journal prompts help you reflect, work through essential issues, and record what you have learned in writing.
- **Group Activities**: These activities allow you to explore concepts and ideas further by interacting with others in your study group, workshop, or classroom.
- **Application**: This section provides strategies for applying what you have learned in your school.

This guide was written to help facilitators lead principals through the contents of a very important and practical book. A foremost goal for facilitators is to enable principals not only to read and understand the contents of the book, but also to *use* the information learned in their own schools.

1

Chapter 1: Why Look at Great?
Chapter 2: It's People, Not Programs

Key Concepts

- ★ Although principals must have a strong knowledge base in their field, what they *know* about being a school principal is subordinate in importance to what they *do* as a school principal.
- ★ The perspective of *What Great Principals Do Differently* is threefold, based on research findings examining effective school leadership, observations at and consultations with many schools and school systems, and the personal core beliefs that guided Whitaker's own work as a successful school principal.
- ★ We can always learn from observing what great principals do. Eliminating inappropriate choices does not help as much as identifying good ideas used by successful educators.
- ★ By studying our most effective school leaders, we examine where they focus their attention, how they spend their time and energy, and what guides their decisions.
- ★ No matter how good our most effective principals are, they still want to be better.
- ★ No program inherently leads to school improvement. It is the people who implement sound programs who determine the success of the school. Programs are never the solution and they are never the problem.
- ★ Recognizing the importance of people over programs, great principals recognize that the two primary ways to improve a school are to hire better teachers and to improve the teachers who already work there.
- ★ Great principals realize that teachers—just like students—vary widely in their individual needs and abilities. As a result, no single program will work with the same rate of success for all teachers. Programs are only solutions when they bring out the best in teachers.
- ★ In addition to promoting whole-school growth and improvement initiatives, great principals do everything possible to promote *individual* teacher development.

Discussion Questions

1. What do great principals see when they view their schools and the people in them?

2. Why should we look at what great principals do?

3. In what ways is looking at ineffective principals limited in its value? On the other hand, why must we also study less effective principals and schools when determining what distinguishes those identified as great?

4. As a school principal, what guides the decisions you make each day?

5. What are some ways you can ensure that you recruit and hire the very best teachers? How can you improve the teachers already working at your school?

6. Why do certain programs work so well for some teachers while other teachers using these same programs fail?

Journal Prompt

Think of a program that you have implemented in recent years at your school or that has been implemented at a school with which you are familiar. Which teachers adapted to the change of programs, embracing the new idea and making it work? Did any teachers resist the change? Was the program ultimately deemed a success? What determined whether or not it was successful? What should principals consider before endorsing schoolwide programs for implementation? If such programs are adopted, what can principals do to foster successful implementation and honor individuality among teachers?

Group Activities

It's Not What You Do—It's How You Do It

Beginning on page 5 of the text, Whitaker describes several "programs" that he deems neither a problem nor a solution: open classrooms, assertive discipline, whole language, direct instruction, mission statements, and state standards. Divide the class into several groups of four to six participants each. Ask each group to discuss the relative merits of one or more of the above "programs" or to pick another one not listed above. Participants should discuss how the chosen program can work effectively or ineffectively, sharing any specific examples from their own experience. Have each group report back whether it was the *people* involved or the *program* itself that determined the level of success.

You Don't Say . . .

Distribute the six quotations regarding leadership below, one each to six groups. Allow time for all groups to study and discuss their quotation. Have them discuss how the quotation is in some way connected to the material presented in Chapter 1 and/or Chapter 2 of the text. Ask each group to offer another quotation with which they are familiar—or even create an original sentence—and share their work with the entire group.

> *Leadership should be more participative than directive, more enabling than performing.*
>
> *A good leader inspires others with confidence in him; a great leader inspires them with confidence in themselves.*
>
> *Good leaders make people feel that they're at the very heart of things, not at the periphery. Everyone feels that he or she makes a difference to the success of the organization. When that happens, people feel centered and that gives their work meaning.*
>
> *Good leaders develop through a never-ending process of self-study, education, training, and experience.*
>
> *A good leader is not the person who does things right, but the person who finds the right things to do.*
>
> *Leaders don't force people to follow—they invite them on a journey.*

Application

Think about ways in which you want your school to improve. While you may at first focus on schoolwide improvements, recall Whitaker's research showing that teachers value principals who not only implement whole-school growth proposals, but also are committed to encouraging and supporting staff development for individual teachers. At your school, begin by asking five teachers you respect what they would most like to improve about their current practice or in what areas they would like to grow professionally. Commit to helping these teachers reach their individual self-improvement goals. Continue this practice by finding out what all the teachers in your building would like to "become" during the future years of their professional careers. Perhaps some aspire to administrative careers or would like to try gifted education or move into counseling. Maybe others would like to teach at different grade levels or in different subject areas. Other teachers may desire less dramatic change, wanting only to improve their classroom discipline practices or use performance assessments more effectively. As the school leader, you must recognize the needs of individual teachers in the vital area of teacher development, since this will also lead to overall school improvement.

Notes

2

Chapter 3: Develop an Accurate Sense of Self

Key Concepts

★ Everyone, including principals, would like to be held in high regard by others, but great principals would rather be respected than liked and work accordingly to earn that respect.

★ Having a clear sense of who we are and what we do is a crucial component of effective leadership. The very best principals stay attuned to how they come across to others and continually work to make sure this self-perception is accurate.

★ Some staff members may be unwilling to volunteer direct feedback regarding the performance of their leader. Great leaders, therefore, purposefully seek feedback on their leadership performance from others.

★ Outstanding principals intentionally plan to get out of their office and be visible in classrooms and throughout the school. They make themselves accessible so that others can readily offer comments and provide feedback.

★ Rather than waiting for others to come to them, great leaders spend time visiting with others, proactively learning about issues before they become problems.

★ The best teachers in any school can offer helpful, constructive feedback that will assist principals in improving their leadership skills; therefore, principals should regularly seek feedback from their very best teachers.

★ The most valuable gift a principal can give to teachers is confidence. Principals can do this by helping teachers build their skills and then encouraging and praising when appropriate.

Discussion Questions

1. We have all heard principals say, "My door is always open." What should this look like, in practice, for principals who are sincerely interested in interacting with teachers at the school? How can an effective open-door policy help principals develop an accurate sense of self?

2. According to Whitaker, in what ways should principals strive to think of themselves as "the ice cream truck" for their schools?

3. What does Whitaker find interesting about surveys that teachers and principals complete about the principal's effectiveness? What conclusion does he draw?

4. Describe the difference between faculty meetings at schools with great principals and meetings at schools with ineffective principals. What are some ways great principals make the most of faculty meetings?

5. Why is it so important for principals to listen to their best teachers and regularly seek their input and feedback?

Journal Prompt

In his presentations to teachers and educational leaders, Whitaker frequently suggests that the greatest gift that a principal can give teachers is confidence and that—in turn—the greatest gift teachers can give their students is confidence. He makes the same suggestion in this chapter also, a chapter devoted to having an accurate sense of self. Think of leaders with whom or for whom you have worked, or even national leaders in whom you have a great deal of confidence. What is it about these leaders that makes you confident in their ability to lead? How do they instill confidence in those they are attempting to lead? Do they appear to have an accurate self-perception, aware of their strengths and weaknesses? In what ways can asking for honest, constructive feedback regarding your own job performance provide you with more confidence in your leadership abilities? How can you help teachers with whom you work to have more confidence in their abilities to lead their students to success?

Group Activities

Getting in Tune

Whitaker states that both effective and ineffective principals view themselves similarly, but that teachers describe effective and ineffective principals very differently. To follow up on this finding, have study group participants work in groups of two to five to self-assess certain leadership practices, discuss individual responses, determine how well their own responses compare with responses of teachers at their respective schools, and then analyze results, sharing areas of celebration and possible growth.

First, have each member of the small group complete the following leadership survey, adapted from *Cornerstones of Strong Schools: Practices for Purposeful Leadership* (Zoul & Link, 2008).[1] Then ask participants to circle responses for which they assigned a score of 4, a trait that is characteristic of them *nearly all the time*. Next, ask them to highlight any statements for which they assigned themselves a score of 1, a trait that is *rarely characteristic* of them. Have group members share their responses within the groups, noting similarities and differences they discover and sharing specific reasons why they answered as they did.

As a culminating activity, challenge those participants who serve as a principal or assistant principal to have teachers at their school complete the survey anonymously, basing their answers on *their* perception of the leader for each of the forty-five indicators. Study group participants should then compare their self-assessment responses to the responses of the teachers at their school. Are there any indicators that teachers scored significantly higher or lower than leaders did themselves? Ask participants to reflect on their self-assessment as well as the responses of their teachers, identifying at least two or three indicators they will target as growth areas for the future. At a subsequent session of the study group, ask several participants to share what they learned after comparing their own answers with those of their teachers.

1 Zoul, J., & Link, L. (2008). *Cornerstones of strong schools: Practices for purposeful leadership*. New York, NY: Routledge.

Leadership Self-Assessment

Please record your current behaviors, beliefs, actions, and attitudes as they relate to practices of purposeful school leadership. Answer each of the following questions using the scale provided. Indicate what you *actually* do—not what you think you *should* do. Don't overthink your answers—go with your first instinct. Be as honest as possible. Do not try to make yourself look good; do not be overly critical. In either case, you'll only be fooling yourself.

4 = Is characteristic of me *nearly all the time*
3 = Is *usually* characteristic of me
2 = Is *sometimes* characteristic of me
1 = Is *rarely* characteristic of me

____ 1. I inquire regularly and often.

____ 2. I remain positive in the midst of anxiety and change.

____ 3. I am an active participant in my school community.

____ 4. I reveal my beliefs through my actions.

____ 5. I have explicit conversations with teachers about their performance.

____ 6. I am equipped to anticipate needs.

____ 7. I routinely spend time in classrooms.

____ 8. I design purposeful and proactive communication with teachers and school community stakeholders.

____ 9. I promote a sense of well-being among my faculty and staff.

____ 10. I involve teachers in all aspects of the school's functioning.

____ 11. I regularly recognize and address school failures.

____ 12. I consciously set a positive emotional tone.

____ 13. I foster mutual respect.

____ 14. I am receptive to negative feedback.

____ 15. I am committed to and make decisions based on a set of ideals and beliefs.

____ 16. I am easily accessible.

____ 17. I create structures to promote and sustain professional conversation.

____ 18. I model the expectations I have of others.

____ 19. I use my school's mission, values, and beliefs to monitor progress.

____ 20. I have high levels of infectious energy.

____ 21. I acknowledge significant events in the lives of teachers.

____ 22. I hold teachers accountable for student achievement.

____ 23. I consciously choose to spend minimal time in my office.

____ 24. I am tuned in to my school's undercurrents.

____ 25. I build the capacity for open dialogue among teachers.

____ 26. I develop common language and common work among my faculty.

____ 27. I often solicit and readily act on feedback.

____ 28. I always engage and respond with timely care.

____ 29. I regularly recognize and celebrate school accomplishments.

____ 30. I strive for consensus.

____ 31. I am the driving force behind major initiatives.

____ 32. I ensure that my school's mission, values, and beliefs are a reflection of all school stakeholders.

____ 33. I communicate and articulate effectively.

____ 34. I often include teachers in analytical and reflective conversations.

____ 35. I listen intently.

____ 36. I regularly attend an array of extracurricular events.

____ 37. I use teams of teachers for decision-making.

____ 38. I am an active participant in my school's core work.

____ 39. I regularly recognize, celebrate, and tap talent among my faculty and staff.

____ 40. I regularly share my beliefs with all school stakeholders.

____ 41. I inspire others to accomplish goals that seem beyond their grasp.

____ 42. I monitor my actions and words.

____ 43. I have frequent contact with students and teachers.

____ 44. I am aware of and respond to the needs of teachers.

____ 45. I systematically recognize and celebrate the accomplishments of students.

Who We Are; What We Do

On page 16, Whitaker states, "A clear sense of who we are and what we do is a crucial component of effective leadership." Arrange participants in groups of three to six. Have each group spend ten minutes brainstorming on a sheet of paper as many descriptions as they can for "who we are"—that is, the roles that a principal assumes (e.g., instructional leader, change agent, evaluator). Next, have each group review the list and reach consensus on the five most important "who we are" roles, writing each of these roles on a separate sheet of chart paper.

Then, have groups brainstorm everything that a principal can and should "do" to fulfill each of these five roles, listing these actions on the respective chart paper. Afterwards, have each group report to the whole group the five roles they considered most important for school principals, along with actions effective principals should take to be effective in each role.

Determine how many different roles were identified (combining roles that may have been named differently but include the same or similar actions). Reassign participants into different groups, one for each role (i.e., if there are nine different roles, regroup participants into nine new groups). If the number of roles is too large for the number of participants, you may assign two roles to each group).

In these new groups, ask participants to examine the role they have been assigned along with the actions necessary to fulfill the role effectively. Have each group create three to five questions or criteria that they could include on a survey of a principal's effectiveness in this area (the facilitator may want the groups to agree on the type of format to be used for the survey questions, such as a 1–5 scale or "Rarely–Sometimes–Often" responses). Collect the questions and compile them into a survey for participants to use in their schools. Provide this document to all participants at the next session, inviting them to have the teachers at their school complete the survey so that study group participants can reflect on their level of effectiveness in each of the areas identified as critically important by the groups.

Notes

Application

In this chapter, Whitaker emphasizes his belief that principals must be visible in classrooms for a variety of reasons, including as a way to solicit input from those in the school setting regarding their own job performance. Many effective principals schedule "no-office" days, going so far as to hang signs on their doors stating that they are "In Classrooms Learning Today." Whitaker encourages such examples of purposefully planning to be out of the office and in classrooms instead.

Although most educational leaders would agree that principals should be visible throughout the campus as often as possible, effective principals also find ways to create an "inviting attitude" about drop-in visits to their office when, indeed, that is where they are. In fact, Whitaker begins the chapter with the heading "Is Your Door Open?" Think about ways that principals can go beyond the "My door is always open" cliché in order to encourage teachers to stop by and offer "drive-by " feedback. For example, consider scheduling an occasional day (maybe once a month) when you remain in your office all day, with the caveat that you are inviting teachers to drop in throughout the day to talk informally. Offer snacks and beverages for teachers outside your office door, encouraging teachers to help themselves and come in to talk. Let teachers know well in advance that you will be hosting such an event and that you are seeking honest feedback. You might consider suggesting in advance of "The Principal Is In Day " these three questions as a way of initiating conversations: (1) What is one thing we are really good at here at our school? (2) What is one thing we need to get better at? (3) What is one thing I can do as principal to help us get better at it?

Notes

3

Chapter 4: Who Is the Variable?

Key Concepts

- ★ Effective principals understand that just as teachers are the variables in the classroom most responsible for students' success, principals are the variables most responsible for the school's success.
- ★ Effective principals make teachers fully aware of the impact they have in their own classrooms. As the leader, the principal helps teachers take responsibility for their own classrooms, but also accepts a higher level of responsibility herself.
- ★ Research shows that effective principals view themselves as responsible for all aspects of their school, while less effective principals blame outside influences for problems in their schools and feel they have no control over outcomes.
- ★ If everyone looks in the mirror when asking "Who is the variable?" we will have made tremendous strides toward school improvement.

? Discussion Questions

1. When the students of our best teachers fail, these teachers typically blame themselves. How does this concept of accepting responsibility apply to school principals?

2. In what key way do effective principals differ from less effective principals in terms of how they view their role?

3. How can principals help teachers take responsibility for student performance in their classrooms?

4. How do effective and less effective principals react when faced with obstacles beyond their direct control, such as budget reductions?

5. Why might parents choose to send their children to a school that has just appointed an outstanding principal to lead a mediocre teaching staff over a school with a strong teaching staff but an ineffective principal?

Notes

Journal Prompt

This chapter stresses as a key idea that what makes the difference between two schools is not a "what" at all, but instead a "who." That is, teachers and principals are the true variables in schools. They have the power to make a difference in the lives of students, each other, and their schools. Consider the hypothetical scenario described on page 21 of the text regarding the two schools. How would you, as the outstanding principal with a weak faculty, take immediate action to begin making this the better of the two schools? Keeping in mind the two-year timeline suggested in the premise, discuss how you would improve the teaching staff and the school's performance overall.

Group Activities

Expectations for Everyone

According to a study cited by the author, effective principals view themselves as responsible for all aspects of their school. While all principals have high expectations for their teachers, great principals also have extremely high expectations for themselves. Working in groups of two to five, have participants reexamine the issue of expectations for principals from the perspective of students, teachers, and parents. What are a few expectations for which all stakeholders should hold all principals accountable? Have each group, as principals, commit to adhering to these expectations by drafting "We will" statements—for example, "As principals, we will treat all members of our school community with dignity and respect." Ask each group to write five "We will" statements to which they would expect themselves and other principals to adhere. Ask each group to share their list, recording answers on the board, overhead, chart paper, or computer screen. Then poll the entire class on which are the five most important statements.

Who Is Responsible? Look In the Mirror

The author suggests that effective principals view themselves as responsible for all aspects of their schools. As we all know, the demands upon principals are exhaustive and seem to be increasing every year. Principals are expected to fulfill numerous responsibilities, including

- supporting the school's vision
- emphasizing the belief that the schools are for learning
- valuing human resources
- being a skilled communicator and listener
- being proactive rather than reactive
- taking risks

Place each of the six headings above on a piece of chart paper. Divide participants into six groups, assigning each group one of the above areas of a principal's responsibility. Ask groups to brainstorm ways they might act on these responsibilities, adding their ideas to the corresponding chart. Post these on the walls of the room, spreading them out as much as possible. Ask each group to do a gallery stroll, spending five minutes at each chart and adding any further ideas they might have for each area. Then, give each participant six adhesive dots and direct them to place one dot on each of the six charts next to the idea they deem most useful, applicable, and important. Once all participants have placed their six dots on the charts, discuss results with the entire group.

Application

Take some time to compare your school to a neighboring school according to some measurable criterion (attendance, test scores, discipline data, etc.). Try to identify an area in which your school might be performing below the level of the comparison school. First, list all the outside factors beyond your control that may (or may not) play a role in the difference between your school's performance and that of the comparison school. Next, decide on what you can control that might improve your own school's performance. Share your thoughts with other leaders at your school and devise a plan focused on improving your school in this targeted area.

Notes

4

Chapter 5: Treat Everyone with Respect, Every Day, All the Time

Key Concepts

- ★ One of the hallmarks of effective principals is how they treat people: with dignity and respect each and every day.
- ★ If we, as principals, treat a student or staff member rudely, that person will never forget it, nor will anyone who witnessed our rudeness.
- ★ Teachers know the difference between right and wrong and want their principals to deal with their irresponsible peers—but in an appropriate and professional manner.
- ★ Our behaviors as principals are much more obvious to all with whom we come in contact than our beliefs. The principal who sets a positive tone can influence the interactions of everyone in the school.
- ★ A key responsibility of an effective leader is to create a positive atmosphere.
- ★ Praise can be a powerful motivator and reinforcer, if used properly. Used correctly, it is impossible to praise too much.
- ★ Principals who consistently model their expectations regarding how people should be treated encourage everyone in the school community to do the same.

Discussion Questions

1. What must principals do to keep the best teachers on their side when dealing with other teachers who are ineffective?

2. Why is it so important for principals to treat all teachers in a dignified and respectful manner each and every day?

3. What is the one central concept Whitaker identifies as key to using praise effectively? Why is this so important?

4. What are some reasons principals give for not praising teachers? What are possible responses to these reasons?

5. Whitaker suggests that how often we praise others is a choice and that whenever we choose to do so, at least two people feel better. Who are these two people? Discuss how the entire school can subsequently benefit as a result of this simple act.

Notes

Journal Prompt

Write about a time when you lost your temper or patience with a student or teacher at your school. How did you react and how did this make you feel? Did your relationship with this student or teacher change as a result? Whitaker suggests that our real challenge is to treat *everyone* at our school with dignity and respect *every* day. Although seemingly simple, as principals we face a multitude of growing demands and constraints. Why is it still so important to focus on the simple concept of treating our students and teachers with dignity and respect?

Group Activities

Our Cup Runneth Over!

The author emphasizes that focusing on the positive elements of our schools will give us more drive and energy as we face our daily work. Divide the class into groups of three to five. Give each group a piece of chart paper with a large cup or glass drawn on it and a package of sticky notes. Participants are to fill their cup with examples of great things happening in their schools. Have participants write brief thoughts and descriptions on the sticky notes and place them in the cup until each cup is filled with positive, productive things happening in the schools. Allow time for individuals to share within their groups. Then, have each group choose and present its top five positive ideas to the entire group. Post these charts for all to read and discuss.

Raise the Praise—Effectively

The author reminds us of the power of praise. Praise should be specific, clear, sincere, and immediate. When praising, make sure to use nonjudgmental language. The key is to express your own feelings in the form of an "I" statement, instead of making a judgment about other people or their work with a "You" statement. For example, say "I respect the way you lead your team" rather than "You are a good teacher"; say "I was impressed with the way you ran the meeting" rather than "You ran the meeting well."

Ask each participant to rate the statements on the next page according to the guidelines provided. After individuals have completed the exercise, have them share their answers with a partner in the class.

Recognizing Effective Praise

Instructions: Place an "E" next to examples of effective praise and an "I" next to examples of ineffective praise. Reword examples of ineffective praise to make them effective praise. Discuss with group members your thoughts about each statement. Share ways that ineffective statements can be improved.

____ 1. I'm glad you remembered to bring your class lists to the meeting. That was good thinking.

____ 2. I appreciate that you remembered to bring your emergency folder. I hope you won't forget next time.

____ 3. For a first-year teacher, you did very well.

____ 4. The room looks really nice. Your bulletin board is meaningful to your unit.

____ 5. Well, now you look much more professional without the baggy sweat pants.

____ 6. I hear you're helping Mr. Smith with his science lessons. That's nice. I am sure he appreciates your encouragement.

____ 7. It was so nice when you ran the awards assembly last year. Could you do that again?

____ 8. (To a teacher who has just presented at a faculty meeting) Good job!

____ 9. Learning new technology is difficult. I'm glad you are trying.

____ 10. Ms. Jones, your students were much better behaved today than at the last assembly.

Notes

Application

On page 29, Whitaker notes several reasons that principals and teachers give for not praising those with whom they work. Make the time during the next five school days to praise at least five different students and five different teachers. For the students, the praise should be in the form of a phone call to parents praising a specific behavior or accomplishment or a postcard or handwritten note sent home in the mail. For teachers, the praise might take the form of a positive note placed in a teacher 's mailbox or a card sent to the teacher through the mail, letting them know how much your school values their work. Report back at the next session whether the time invested was worthwhile based on the reactions you received.

Notes

5

Chapter 6: Be the Filter

Key Concepts

- ★ Effective principals realize that they are the filters for the day-to-day reality of the school and that their behavior sets the tone for all.
- ★ Principals must serve as a filter for which information is shared with teachers and other stakeholders. By sparing others unnecessary bad news, the principal creates a more productive environment.
- ★ The principal is the most significant influence upon the entire school; the principal's focus becomes the school's focus. Principals must keep their attention on issues that matter rather than diverting effort and energy to trivial annoyances.
- ★ Great principals use regular faculty meetings as staff development opportunities.
- ★ Regardless of the purpose, content, or focus of a faculty meeting, the principal's additional challenge should be to have teachers leave the meeting more excited about teaching tomorrow than they were today.
- ★ Great principals understand that perceptions can become reality. One of the best ways to alter negative perceptions is to provide other perceptions.
- ★ Consciously or not, principals *decide* the tone of the school.

❓ Discussion Questions

1. How do the principal's responses to questions and situations affect teachers in the school?

2. How should principals determine which information they should filter out and not share with staff members?

3. What is the result when a principal shares with a teacher an unpleasant situation that he had with an angry parent?

4. What factors determine whether the teachers at a school work to please the principal or work against her?

5. How can principals work to change perceptions of those teachers who complain about their students and other problems at their schools?

Notes

Journal Prompt

Whitaker offers several examples of situations in which leaders should "filter out" a minor annoyance. Consider the examples offered, including "thumping," the angry parent, and the "potentially bad legislation." Discuss in writing other negative incidents you face each day that can be filtered out and not passed along to teachers. At times, of course, principals must share significant negative information with teachers. What is the most effective way to share such news? How can a principal openly discuss such news with teachers without shifting their energy to unproductive worrying?

Group Activities

Circle of Friends

Arrange the group into two circles, one inside the other, with the participants in the inner circle facing the people in the outer circle. Have the people in the inner circle relate an example of negativity at their school. The person in the outer circle should listen carefully and offer suggestions for dealing with this difficult, negative person and/or situation. After five minutes, have the inner circle rotate three places to the right. Repeat the activity, this time with the person in the outer circle sharing a negative scenario. Repeat one or two additional times. Then, as a whole class, share what was learned. Did most participants share similar stories? What examples of negativity are principals faced with regularly? What were the most useful strategies for dealing with negative people and situations?

Setting the Tone

Principals, consciously or not, decide the tone of the school. Here are ten suggestions that principals can use to set the tone. Have participants review the ten ideas with a partner or small group and then list two or three tangible ways to implement each suggestion.

1. **Support new teachers.**
   Nearly one-third of new U.S. teachers leave the profession during their first three years. Almost half leave during the first five. The price of high turnover is enormous in terms of money, productivity, and morale.
2. **Clue into climate.**
   What happens at faculty meetings? What traditions and ceremonies do teachers and staff have available to celebrate successes? These are elements of school climate, the underlying attitudes and expectations of your employees. Climate affects morale enormously.
3. **Empower teachers and staff.**
   People are happiest when they have some control over their work environment. Autocratic, top-down leadership tends to quash teacher and employee morale.
4. **Recognize and reward teachers and staff.**
   Let teachers know they're doing a good job. Recognizing their achievements publicly goes a long way toward making them feel appreciated.
5. **Don't ignore administrator morale.**
   Unhappy administrators hurt morale.
6. **Deal with student discipline.**
   Disruptive student behavior damages teacher morale and leads some teachers to leave the profession. New teachers in particular have trouble with classroom management, and teachers who leave say they don't feel adequately backed up by principals when it comes to disciplining individual students.
7. **Treat teachers like professionals.**
   Teachers need professional development and time to collaborate with colleagues. If they know they are expected to be continuous learners, like their students, they see themselves as professionals.
8. **Ask employees what's going on.**
   Gathering employee input, whether through informal chat sessions or by a written school survey, gives the staff a chance to be heard on important issues. It also can alert administrators and others to potential problems.

9. **Keep facilities tidy**.
   Teachers who work every day in crumbling, dirty, and neglected buildings are bound to feel that their work isn't especially valued.
10. **Develop emotional understanding**.
    Teachers need to feel emotional support from the person for whom they work. Being empathetic and appreciating a well-done job are just two ways principals can provide emotional support to their employees. Good leaders do this to help teachers work at their highest levels.

Application

Upon returning to your school, make a conscious decision to filter out negative situations that you face, whether they come from outside or within the school. Respond cheerfully to any staff member who asks how you are doing. Politely redirect any negative comments made by a staff member. Brag about your students and teachers each day to anyone who will listen. Tell students at the end of each day that you can't wait to return to school tomorrow because you are so excited about what they will be learning. After doing this for several consecutive days, record in your study guide any changes you noticed in your own perspective or in that of the students and teachers at your school.

Notes

6

Chapter 7: Teach, Don't Tell

Key Concepts

- ★ Outstanding principals know that their primary role is to teach the teachers. Great principals focus on students by focusing on teachers.
- ★ If we want our teachers to do better, we must teach them how. We cannot expect teachers to do better if they do not know a better way.
- ★ Our students benefit from observing teachers working together successfully. Great principals find ways for teachers to collaborate in order to improve school and student performance.
- ★ Great principals do not let the many demands upon their time prevent them from improving teacher effectiveness.
- ★ Effective principals take time to get into the classrooms of troubled teachers and help build their skills.
- ★ The more time that principals spend building the skills of their teachers, the less they are drained by reacting to the results of ineffective teaching practices.
- ★ One of the principal's most important jobs is getting into classrooms. When teachers see the principal in their classrooms, they see how he expects them to interact with students.
- ★ Great principals do not let teachers who drag their feet keep others from making a difference.
- ★ Collaboration among classroom teachers is one of the most basic and effective ways to improve instruction. Since our goal is to help all teachers to become as good as our best teachers, a good place to start is by giving everyone a chance to observe each other. When we use our best teachers as positive role models, we multiply their productivity and help other teachers improve their own performance.

Discussion Questions

1. Students are the most important people in the school. How can principals best help their students?

2. If it is true, as Whitaker surmises, that all teachers do the best they can in managing their classrooms, what must we do as principals to help them improve if they are struggling in this critical area?

3. Most principals realize that most discipline referrals they receive emanate from the classrooms of only a few teachers. What should principals do to address this problem proactively rather than reactively?

4. Why is it important for teachers to get out of their own classrooms and observe each other teaching?

5. According to Whitaker, what is a potential obstacle a principal faces in getting teachers to observe each other? How do great principals deal with this obstacle?

Notes

Journal Prompt

Describe three of the best teachers at your school. What makes them stand out? What qualities do they have that you wish all teachers at your school had? Think about three other teachers who might benefit from observing these three superstars in action. Would they be able to improve their own performance after observing their colleagues? Would the superstar teachers learn something through this process as well? Approached carefully, would both the superstar and mediocre teacher be willing to observe in each other 's classrooms? In what ways could this interchange benefit your students and improve your school?

 **Group Activities**

You Oughta Be in Pictures!

The facilitator could make a compilation of clips from several movies to enhance this activity, but it is probably not absolutely necessary since most educators have seen several of these movies. In either case, discuss these and other movies that focus on an educator as a central character. Make a list of common characteristics that the teachers in the movies possess. Have participants share with a partner some similarities between the teacher character in one of the films and a teacher at their own school or a teacher they had during their own education.

- *Blackboard Jungle*
- *Dangerous Minds*
- *Dead Poets Society*
- *Goodbye, Mr. Chips*
- *Mr. Holland's Opus*
- *October Sky*
- *Stand and Deliver*
- *Teacher*
- *To Sir with Love*
- *Up the Down Staircase*

Featuring Our Own Teachers

Have participants work with other principals of schools at the same level (elementary, middle, high school) to develop a plan that can be implemented at their schools whereby teachers are given opportunities to observe other teachers. Ask participants to consider how they will get the least effective teachers into the most effective teachers' classrooms without hurt feelings. Also, have them discuss if funds will be needed, what kind of preparation and follow-up teachers would be required to do, whether to encourage or require some sort of feedback or share session after the observation, and other questions that might arise. Have each group share their thoughts with the entire group.

Notes

Application

For the next five school days, make it a point to get into classrooms throughout the school building as much as possible. You might even gather some paperwork you need to complete and bring it into several classrooms to work on throughout the day. While you are visiting and working in classrooms, take note of what students are learning. As you walk around classrooms while students are working independently, ask them quietly, "What are you learning?" Make mental records of students' responses. Share five of the most interesting responses with your staff via an email. If you notice something in a classroom that seems to be interfering with student learning, ask the teacher later for his own thoughts regarding your observation and offer ideas for improvement.

Notes

7

Chapter 8: Hire Great Teachers

Key Concepts

- ★ A principal's single most precious commodity is an opening on the teaching staff. The quickest way to improve your school is to hire great teachers at every opportunity. Great principals hire teachers who are better than those teachers they are replacing.
- ★ In hiring new teachers, great principals want the school to become more like the new teacher instead of the other way around. Hiring teachers who will "fit right in" should not be the principal's primary goal.
- ★ Great principals hire dynamic teachers and strive to keep them that way. They look for teachers who will be not only great in the classroom but also influential in the school.
- ★ Many of the qualities great principals look for—love of students, positive attitude, congenial personality—are more inherent than learned. Great principals, therefore, value such overall traits over specific technique.
- ★ Highly talented teachers will thrive wherever the principal puts them and will make the school better.
- ★ There must be no pecking order in schools. Great principals make decisions about teachers based on each individual's effectiveness and contributions rather than seniority.
- ★ New teacher induction should start during the interviewing process through skillful, strategic questioning and establishing expectations.

Discussion Questions

1. Why is hiring great teachers so monumentally important?

2. Why does Whitaker downplay the importance of hiring teachers who are "a good match"?

3. What is the essential variable in hiring new teachers? What factors are secondary in importance to this core indicator of future success?

4. How can principals begin to send the message that there is no pecking order and that effectiveness is valued over seniority?

5. In what ways can a principal informally begin the process of induction during the interview?

6. How can principals discreetly let new teachers know which colleagues they should choose as role models?

Journal Prompt

Whitaker states that he would rather hire a new teacher with "a jarful of talent and a thimbleful of technique than the other way around" (p. 49). Reflect on this statement and what it means to you. Do you agree or disagree? What constitutes "talent" when looking for great teachers? What constitutes "technique"? How heavily should you value factors such as advanced degrees and years of experience?

Group Activities

Top Teaching Traits

Have each participant brainstorm a list of ten traits to look for when hiring new teachers. Next, have participants discuss their lists with a partner. Regroup participants into groups of three or four. Distribute the following list of teacher traits and ask each group to rank them in order from 1 to 15, with 1 being the most essential characteristic of a new teacher. Have each group report back to the large group and compare rankings. Discuss any glaring difference—or similarities—among the various group rankings.

- flexibility
- organization
- ability to build success into the class
- ability to communicate clearly
- ability to create a pleasant atmosphere
- ability to differentiate instruction
- effective classroom management
- enthusiasm
- high expectations
- content knowledge
- good people skills (with students, staff, parents)
- ability to pace instruction
- ability to ask effective questions
- good attitude
- ability to teach actively

Induction Starts at the Interview

The author suggests that we need to begin the induction process as early as during the interview (once we have determined that the teaching candidate is a strong prospect). Given the above list of fifteen traits that many principals find desirable when seeking new teachers, the key is to (1) ask probing questions that ensure that we are learning whether the candidate possesses these characteristics and (2) begin the induction process by setting expectations regarding each of these traits. Ask pairs of participants to take turns role-playing the interview scenario, focusing on one key trait at a time. The "interviewer " should attempt to ask realistic questions aimed at discerning whether the "candidate" possesses the identified trait. The "candidate" should answer the questions in a way that she feels would most likely be a favorable reply. The "interviewer " should start inducting the "candidate" by letting her know his expectations regarding how she should display the trait if she became a teacher at the school.

Application

Upon returning to your school, jot down the names of five "superstar" teachers at your school. Try to pick teachers at various grade levels and/or in various subject areas. List five or six characteristics that make each one an outstanding teacher and member of your school community. From these five lists, choose the traits you listed most often.

Before beginning the next part of this activity, be very aware of the school dynamic you work in. Keep this exercise focused on the desirable traits and characteristics; do not mention specific teachers' names. Your goal is to improve your entire staff. Overtly making some teachers look better than the rest can cause ill will. You can always privately let these teachers know how much you value their expertise and performance.

Continue this activity by writing a paragraph (again, without identifying the teachers' names) about each trait you value most. Share these paragraphs with your staff in a memo or email, perhaps citing examples you notice each day as you visit classrooms throughout your school. In addition to discussing the general traits of these educators, pinpoint two or three specific practices these master teachers exhibit in their classrooms that you would like all members of your faculty to learn.

Notes

8

Chapter 9: Recruiting and Retaining Talent

Key Concepts

- ★ The main goal we should have when hiring new teachers is that we want our school to become more like the new teacher, not to have the new teacher become like the school.
- ★ Many new teachers want to make a difference more than they want to make money. They want to matter, and they will have that opportunity at your school.
- ★ We must make sure prospective teachers understand that we do not hire new teachers to fall in line. We hire new teachers to form new lines.
- ★ We should not hire people to provide what we have; we should hire them to provide what we do not have.
- ★ We should hire for talent, not just experience. Talent surpasses experience very quickly if teachers are under the right leadership.
- ★ During the interview, focusing on classroom management is an excellent approach simply because everyone does the best they know how.
- ★ New teachers are one of the most precious commodities in a school. They can bring energy, enthusiasm, and ideas.
- ★ Teachers need to feel supported and one way they feel supported is when they see their principal regularly, including in their classroom frequently.
- ★ People do not just quit their jobs, they quit their bosses. An easy way to differentiate yourself from the masses as a leader is by being more supportive, more visible, and more concerned.
- ★ Leaders need to carefully think through the connections that we encourage when we make decisions like mentor assignments. We might be creating their peer group, and we need to visualize in advance if that is the outcome we desire based on who we assign as mentors.
- ★ Leaders must understand the importance of social connectivity and work to link new staff members with as many positive and effective colleagues as possible.
- ★ Effective leaders find ways to support and protect new teachers and work to give them the gift of confidence.

Discussion Questions

1. Why do we want our school to become more like new teachers we hire rather than the other way around?

2. What are some ways we can proactively recruit new teachers when we have openings, even in times of teacher shortages and when we work in remote areas?

3. During the interview, why is it beneficial to ask questions about classroom management? What are some classroom management questions we could pose to teacher candidates?

4. Why is it so important to check references? How can we do this most effectively?

5. Discuss several ways we can make new teachers we hire feel more supported.

Notes

Journal Prompt

When checking references, Whitaker suggests probing more deeply about whether a teacher's current principal would re-hire the person. One suggestion he makes is to ask whether the current principal would actually recruit the teacher. He goes further, asking the principal how many teachers on staff he would actively recruit. Consider the school at which you currently serve. How many of the teachers in place are ones you would actively recruit, those teachers who are so excellent that they make not only their students, but the entire school, better? What is it about these teachers that make them so exceptional? Consider what can be done to recruit similar teachers as well as what can be done to retain these current teachers.

Group Activities

Twenty Questions

Whitaker offers several specific questions (and follow up questions) to ask teaching candidates. Review the following list of additional potential interview questions. In your group, choose the five that you feel are the best. Be prepared to defend your answers:

1. Why did you decide to become a teacher?
2. How would you handle a student who is constantly disruptive or defiant?
3. How do you cultivate positive relationships with your students and create a sense of class community?
4. How do you use data to differentiate instruction and support students identified with specific learning disabilities so all students can learn?
5. How do you support literacy for all students, including English language learners?
6. Do you incorporate collaborative and project-based learning?
7. How do you keep your students engaged and motivated, and how do you promote student voice and choice to help them become self-directed learners?
8. How do you teach 21st-century learners, integrate technology, and guide students to be global citizens?
9. How do you include parents and guardians in their child's education?
10. How do you maintain your own professional development, and what areas would you select for your personal growth?
11. Please tell me the most important thing you know now as an educator that you wish you knew before you began your teaching career.
12. How much do you want to know about your students in order to be most helpful to them?
13. What do you find most frustrating about teaching?
14. How would you get your classroom ready for the first day of school?
15. How do you manage your time to get all your teaching duties done within schedule?
16. What do you like best about teaching?
17. What's the biggest challenge today's students face?
18. Describe a troubling student you've taught and what you've done to get through to them.
19. If the majority of your class failed a test, project or assignment, what would you do?
20. We try to hire teachers who are so outstanding that when we hire them, we want the school to become more like them rather than the other way around. What it is something about you that is so special that we would want the rest of the staff to emulate?

What Do You Need?

Whitaker notes the importance of having effective mentoring programs in place. One aspect of effective mentoring is ensuring that new teachers are placed with mentors who will influence the new teacher to grow and remain a positive influence within the school community. Once an appropriate mentor is assigned to a new teacher, we should identify activities for the mentor and his/her "mentee" to engage in. In your group, review the following possible mentor-mentee activities. Which ones are most important in your opinion? What five activities would you add to this list?

1. Keep a reflective journals—what worked; student gains; concerns; feelings. Review periodically with the mentor teacher.
2. Attend a professional learning event together.

3. Discuss a lesson over dinner.
4. Celebrate mutual teaching successes and learning—share student work.
5. Discuss grading, assessment, and report card marks as well as evaluation and feedback strategies.
6. Explore the school library/media center and equipment together.
7. Plan parent-teacher conferences.
8. Read a professional book together.
9. Take a video of lessons and review together

Notes

Application

Citation for this: Podsen, I., & Denmark, V. M. (2006). *Coaching and Mentoring First Year and Student Teachers (2nd Edition)*. New York, NY: Routledge.

Use this new teacher needs assessment with five or more of the most recent teacher hires at your school. Ask each of them to complete it, pretending that they are just beginning their teaching career as they respond. Based on the results, identify what themes emerge as being areas that most teachers will need the most assistance with at the outset of their careers. Are there other items you would add to this assessment?

Needs Assessment for Protégés

Please choose the response that most closely indicates your level of need for assistance in the area described.
Possible Responses

A. Little or no need for assistance in this area
B. Some need for assistance in this area
C. Moderate need for assistance in this area
D. High need for assistance in this area
E. Very high need for assistance in this area

1. _____Finding out what is expected of me as a teacher
2. _____Communicating with the principal
3. _____Communicating with other teachers
4. _____Communicating with parents
5. _____Organizing and managing my classroom
6. _____Maintaining student discipline
7. _____Obtaining instructional resources and materials
8. _____Planning for instruction
9. _____Managing my time and work
10. _____Diagnosing student needs
11. _____Evaluating student progress
12. _____Motivating students
13. _____Assisting students with special needs
14. _____Planning for individual differences among students
15. _____Understanding the curriculum
16. _____Completing administrative paperwork
17. _____Using a variety of teaching methods
18. _____Facilitating group discussions
19. _____Grouping for effective instruction

20. _____Administering tests
21. _____Understanding the school system's teacher evaluation process
22. _____Understanding my legal rights and responsibilities as a teacher
23. _____Dealing with stress
24. _____Dealing with contractual and ATA-related issues
25. _____Becoming aware of special services provided by the school district

Notes

9

Chapter 10: Understand the Dynamics of Change

Key Concepts

- ★ The best leaders never forget that their ongoing focus is improvement, not perfection, and continue to ask themselves and their teachers, "How can we get better?"
- ★ Leading can be a daunting task, but the best school leaders understand how to navigate the change dynamic so that all students can have the outstanding school they deserve.
- ★ Implementing change successfully in schools means changing the school culture—the collective beliefs and values that influence policies and practices in the school. Great principals know it is quite possible to change a school culture quickly if they lead and communicate change initiatives effectively.
- ★ Great principals know that effective change is up to them. With a purpose, plan, and persistence, they can make a difference in a remarkably short period of time.
- ★ When it comes to implementing change, great principals learn to rely on the very best people in the organization. These staff members know how to come up with effective strategies and will work hard to pursue change that matters.
- ★ Rather than hunkering down when dramatic change is afoot, the very best leaders take a much more forward-thinking approach. They look beyond the storm of funding cuts and other challenges and work to make sure the essential pillars are still standing after the storm passes.
- ★ During turbulent times, great principals do everything in their power to reassure their superstars that everything will work out. At the same time, they make it clear to less stellar staff that their workload will increase and they will be held accountable.

Discussion Questions

1. What is Whitaker's definition of "school culture"?

2. How are school culture and change directly related?

3. What is the difference between changing a school's climate and changing its culture?

4. In the anecdote Whitaker shares, how did "Aunt Sally" change the culture of the family dinner table? What applications do you see for principals hoping to change their school's culture?

5. How do some principals turn challenges into opportunities?

6. What does Whitaker mean when he suggests that great principals "never see the before"?

Journal Prompt

At times it seems as if change is the only constant in our noble profession of education. Think about change initiatives that you have been a part of in a school or school district, either as a teacher or as an administrator. List at least five major changes that have affected you during your career in education. Choose one change that was implemented smoothly and that endured over time. Then choose a change initiative that failed altogether or failed to prove lasting. What were the differences in the two scenarios? How did the school culture and climate affect each? How did the very best teachers at the school respond to both situations? How were the two change initiatives communicated to teachers at the school? What can others learn from the successful change as well as the unsuccessful example? What are the two most important points Whitaker makes about understanding the dynamics of change in this chapter?

Group Activities

The CORE of Change

In an earlier book (Whitaker & Zoul, 2008),[1] the authors write about four factors that impact overall school success, including implementing change initiatives effectively. These factors, represented by the acronym CORE, are: Communication, Observation, Relationships, and Expectations. Initiate a discussion with participants about how these four words are related to changing the culture of a school and what leaders can do in each of the four areas.

Divide the group into four teams. Give each team an envelope with one of the four CORE factors written on the front. In addition, provide each team with a stack of index cards. Give participants two minutes to write down on the index cards ways a school leader can demonstrate this factor to successfully change the school culture (depending on the number of team members, they may work individually, in pairs, or as a whole group). Ask them to write only one idea per index card, with their goal being to generate as many idea cards as they can that represent actions leaders can take to initiate change and establish and maintain positive school cultures.

After two minutes, have each team gather all cards and place them in their envelope. Next, rotate the envelopes from one team to another. Have each team write ideas for their new factor. Repeat the process a third time so that each team will have worked for two minutes on three of the four CORE factors. Then, rotate the envelopes one more time and ask teams to take five minutes as a team to discuss the cards in the envelope and divide them into three different piles as follows: (1) things we already do; (2) things we'd like to start doing right away; (3) things we might consider at some point in the future. After five minutes, ask each team to debrief by sharing with the whole group one item that all or nearly all team members already do and one item that all or nearly all team members would like to consider doing.

Riding a Dead Horse

Refer participants to the following account from Sarason (1996):[2]

Common advice from knowledgeable horse trainers includes the adage "If the horse you're riding dies, get off." This advice seems simple enough, yet people in the education business don't always follow that advice. Instead, they choose from an array of alternatives (see next page).

1. Whitaker, T., & Zoul, J. (2008). *The 4 CORE factors for school success*. New York, NY: Routledge.
2. Sarason, S. B. (1996). *Revisiting "the culture of the school and the problem of change."* New York, NY: Teachers College Press.

- buying a stronger whip
- trying a new bit or bridle
- switching riders
- moving the horse to a new location
- riding the horse for longer periods of time
- saying things like "This is the way we've always ridden this horse"
- appointing a committee to study horses
- arranging to visit other sites where they ride dead horses efficiently
- increasing the standards for riding dead horses
- creating a test for measuring our riding ability
- comparing how we're riding now with how we did it ten or twenty years ago
- complaining about the state of horses these days
- coming up with new styles of riding
- blaming the horse's parents: the problem is in the breeding
- tightening the cinch

This horse story encapsulates what many people think about reform efforts in schools. The alternatives listed allow riders to examine and change superficial aspects of riding and of horses in general, but the horse is still dead. Many reform efforts target the superficial aspects of schools, but disregard the "collective beliefs and values that influence policies and practices within a school" that Whitaker mentions in this chapter.

In small groups of two to five members each, have participants review this list of fifteen practices guaranteed to result in *not* changing the school culture. Ask groups to pick at least three of the items on the list for which they can provide an example from a school where they have worked where a change initiative failed when leaders and/or teachers attempted that approach. Next, ask each group to choose one of these examples and devise an alternate approach that would have yielded more favorable results and enduring change. Ask each group to share their example.

Notes

Application

Upon returning to your school, spend some time thinking about school culture and how it impacts change. Regardless of how much time you may have already devoted to discussing school culture with teachers at your school, plan on devoting a short, but focused amount of time to this important topic again. Either at a scheduled whole-faculty meeting or a fifteen-minute whole-faculty meeting called solely for this purpose, communicate to teachers the importance of school culture. Offer several definitions, including the one in this chapter: "the collective beliefs and values that influence policies and practices within a school." After briefly "teaching" the staff what school culture is, including your preferred definition, suggest that, in addition to school culture, each individual classroom takes on its own culture. Ask teachers to describe the classroom culture they are trying to create, emailing responses to you within a week. Let them know that at the same time you will be working to describe in writing the school culture you are hoping to create, maintain, and strengthen.

After a week, share via an email, weekly memo, newsletter, blog, or some other form of communication in place at your school your own written description of an ideal school culture along with three or four examples of ideal classroom cultures written by your teachers (you will probably choose to share these anonymously). Continue to keep school culture and classroom culture at the forefront of discussions throughout the year and especially as you are implementing changes in the school.

Notes

10

Chapter 11: Standardized Testing
Chapter 12: Focus on Behavior, Then Focus on Beliefs

Key Concepts

- ★ Core issues such as teacher morale, school culture and climate, and student behavior have been central to schools for decades and will remain essential decades from now.
- ★ Great principals focus on enduring core values, spending less time and energy on the hot-button issues that would shift their attention from what really matters.
- ★ Regardless of widely varying beliefs about standardized testing, principals must deal with the reality of testing and behave accordingly. They must shift their focus away from beliefs and center on behaviors.
- ★ Although effective principals do not let standardized testing consume the entire school, they realize that success on standardized tests allows them greater autonomy to do what they believe is best for students.
- ★ Effective principals describe student achievement in much broader terms than less effective principals, listing not only test scores, but also student social skills, behavior, responsibility, involvement in school, and similar characteristics as important components of student success.
- ★ The greatest impediment to change is fear, especially fear of the unknown. Even if a new approach is guaranteed to work, the transition is scary. Great principals convince teachers to change not by persuading them to change their beliefs, but by getting them to change their behaviors.
- ★ By demonstrating strategies for effecting change, principals empower teachers and can reasonably expect them to change their behavior. Effective principals do not waste time or energy trying to persuade everyone that a new way will be better than the old way. They realize that changing behaviors paves the way for changing beliefs.

Discussion Questions

1. What are two key questions we should ask in determining the role of standardized tests? What is the relationship between these two questions?

2. How do great principals manage to get all teachers on the same page regarding standardized testing despite the fact that opinions vary so widely?

3. In the matter of standardized testing—and any other potentially controversial topic—how do the most effective leaders decide to deal with the issue when talking with teachers and other stakeholders?

4. Effective principals realize the risk of making standardized tests and testing standards the center of the school's business. Explain this risk and what should instead guide a principal's decision-making.

5. Why is it more effective and productive for a principal to focus on teachers' behaviors rather than on their beliefs?

6. Explain Whitaker's suggestions in the section "Let's Call Those Parents" in Chapter 12 for getting teachers to initiate regular contacts with parents.

7. Instead of wasting time and energy trying to persuade reluctant teachers to buy into a new system or idea, how do effective principals ensure that teachers become interested and begin to change?

Journal Prompt

In Chapter 12, Whitaker stresses that while great principals respect the beliefs of all teachers, it is often more helpful to focus on behaviors, rather than beliefs, when attempting to implement change. He offers a few examples of teachers' behavior that principals might want to change, including getting teachers to call parents regularly or use praise more frequently. Think of one area at your own school in which you would like to see the vast majority of your teachers change or grow. Describe how getting your teachers to change would improve your school. What can you do to change teachers' behaviors so that this change can be effected?

 **Group Activities**

Two Key Questions

The author maintains that it is time to stop debating the merits of standardized testing and focus instead on educators' behaviors related to the issue of testing. In groups of five or fewer, have participants discuss the two key questions he poses: (1) What should our schools be doing? (2) What do standardized tests measure? Have each group portray its answers pictorially, using a framework similar to that offered in Figures 1 and 2 (pp. 77–78) of the text. Have each group create a Top 10 list of the vitally important things that schools must do that are not measured by standardized testing. Then have each group create another Top 10 list of the most important reasons for schools to demonstrate success on standardized tests. Have groups draw their circles and write their Top 10 lists on chart paper. Ask the groups to present their findings.

Actions Speak Louder Than Words

Arrange participants into groups of three or four. Have them develop and share a skit that illustrates how a teacher, administrator, or student demonstrates through their behavior a positive or negative image or attitude. Look to the example of the teacher who put her hands on her hips and sighed when she was displeased (p. 82). Ask participants to concentrate on and discuss the effects of their body language. Many people do not realize that their actions are speaking much louder than their words!

Notes

Application

Upon returning to your school, list five belief statements regarding education that you think nearly all your teachers would endorse—for example, (1) All kids can learn; (2) The work we do at our school is important; (3) We will not give up on students; (4) Communicating with parents is important; (5) Teacher and student attendance impacts student learning. Try to change these belief statements into value statements or commitments that show what behaviors you and your staff are willing to exhibit to make these beliefs a living reality in your school community. Enlist the support of other leaders at your school in identifying one or two key behaviors that you think most of your teachers would be willing to support, and ask them all to change their behavior to reflect this point of emphasis.

Notes

11

Chapter 13: Loyal to Whom?
Chapter 14: Base Every Decision on Your Best Teachers

Key Concepts

- ★ All principals would like their teachers to be loyal to them. Effective principals expect their teachers to be loyal to the students. Great principals are loyal to their students, to their teachers, and to their school.
- ★ Loyalty means making decisions based on what is best for *all* students. Principals cannot make a decision based on what is best for *one* student at the expense of the other students.
- ★ Effective principals expect teachers to place the needs of their students ahead of their own personal desires, and they expect no less from themselves. Otherwise, they shift their focus from the students to themselves.
- ★ Talented teachers are often strong-willed people who may challenge a principal's decisions and even strongly oppose them. However, if their focus is consistently on the students, perhaps they are right.
- ★ Principals who want to improve their schools will find ways to focus on their best teachers. The best principals base every decision on their best teachers.
- ★ Teachers can be classified as superstars, backbones, and mediocres. Superstars are those teachers whose former students remember them, who are regularly requested by parents, and who are respected by their peers. If they left your school, you would probably not be able to hire other teachers as good to replace them.
- ★ The most effective principals understand that their school will go as far as their best teachers take it; therefore, they value their superstar teachers.
- ★ Effective principals consult their best teachers before attempting to implement change. They have the confidence to seek input in advance of change initiatives and feedback after the fact.
- ★ Effective principals understand that the hardest teacher to move forward is the first one, not the last one. Once the superstars move forward, the backbones will move with them.
- ★ Superstars will always be effective, but if a principal does not value their input, they will limit their influence to their individual classrooms. Principals need their superstars to influence the entire school.
- ★ Effective principals do not issue orders and directives to the entire staff. Instead, they address only those teachers who are creating the problem.

Discussion Questions

1. Why is it more important for teachers to be loyal to their students rather than to the principal?
2. In dealing with staff members, what focus should guide the principal to make the right decision?
3. How can two people both be right even when they vehemently disagree?
4. Why must principals base their decisions on the very best teachers in the school?
5. Typically, what percent of a faculty is comprised of superstar teachers?
6. If the very best teachers do not think something is a good idea, should the principal still proceed with the idea? Why or why not?
7. Why do principals ask all teachers for input? Why do principals ask their superstar teachers for input?
8. Why must principals use discretion in asking their superstar teachers for input?

Journal Prompt

In these chapters, Whitaker discusses why principals should be loyal to students and base their decisions on their very best people. Think about your very best teachers. Are they loyal to their students? How does this loyalty impact your own job as principal? Discuss in writing one or two teachers with whom you consult informally when you are considering whether to implement change or make a significant decision related to the school. Do these teachers tend to offer keen insights? Are they forthright, even if their answers may not be the ones you were hoping for? How do you react to such feedback? Would you still move forward with an idea for change if one or two of your best teachers were opposed?

Group Activities

Decisions, Decisions, Decisions

Divide principals into groups of four or five based on whether they serve at the elementary, middle, or high school level. Have the participants at each level consider their respective scenario:

- **Elementary**: A teacher has proposed that all students remain silent during the first ten minutes of lunch each day.
- **Middle**: A teacher has proposed that the school adopt a "silent transition" policy, whereby students must be silent in the corridors during class changes.
- **High**: A teacher has proposed that the school adopt a "no zero" policy, whereby teachers cannot give the grade of zero for any assignment, but must instead label the assignment "Incomplete" until the student makes up the work.

Ask the groups to decide whether to implement their proposals, considering three important questions in coming to a decision: (1) What is the purpose of the proposal? (2) Will the proposal accomplish this purpose? (3) What would the best teachers at my school think about this change? Have each group report its decision to the entire class, noting whether group members were unanimous.

Spelling It Out

Arrange principals in small groups. Have each group create a definition of loyalty from a principal's perspective. Share and discuss definitions within the entire group. Next, post the following components of loyalty and have the large group compare their definitions with these descriptors.
Loyalty is:

- Being there to help people whenever they need help
- Supporting students and teachers and not laughing at them when they need help
- Keeping a promise or honoring a commitment
- Considering what is best for students despite what you or your teachers may want or need
- Helping someone with a problem as if it were your own
- Being true to yourself and others
- Looking out for the best interests of everyone involved

Reorganize participants into new small groups and ask them to come up with a word or phrase associated with loyalty that begins or incorporates each letter of the word "loyalty" itself. Present on chart paper.

L

O

Y

A

L

T

Y

Application

At every school, principals must decide how to deal with staff members who act inappropriately in trivial situations, creating a problem for the entire school. Whitaker offers an example of teachers who abuse the copy machine, regularly making inordinate numbers of copies. Think of such a situation at your own school. Knowing that issuing edicts to the entire staff to address the indiscretions of a few is counterproductive, what do you do? Call a principal at another school with whom you enjoy a collegial relationship and ask how she handles such situations. Are there times when you have issued schoolwide directives? Share your thoughts and insights gained at the next session.

Notes

12

Chapter 15: In Every Situation, Ask Who Is Most Comfortable and Who Is Least Comfortable

Key Concepts

- ★ All principals face the challenge of balancing rules and guidelines with those times when they need to make exceptions to the established rules.
- ★ All principals must establish internal ground rules for making decisions in such instances. One internal standard that supports effective leadership is to always ask when making decisions, "Who is most comfortable and who is least comfortable in this situation?"
- ★ Principals want those who are uncomfortable to change in a positive direction; they do not want to create an uncomfortable situation for their best teachers.
- ★ Positive staff members will align themselves on the side of the principal when he deals effectively with less positive staff.
- ★ Great principals avoid sending general directives or reminders to all students, teachers, or parents. Instead, they try to approach only those students, teachers, or parents who are responsible for the problem.
- ★ When principals must send out a communication to an entire group, they should focus on the positive people and treat everyone as if they were good. Such notes reinforce good behavior and make those exhibiting noncompliance uncomfortable.
- ★ Teachers should not punish an entire class for the misbehavior of a few students. Principals, too, should follow this guideline.
- ★ Applied consistently, the question, "Who is most comfortable and who is least comfortable?" can bring clarity to a principal's decision-making.

❓ Discussion Questions

1. Why must principals—at times—make decisions that are exceptions to explicit rules and guidelines? When does this situation most often arise?

2. Why does the landlord described in Whitaker's book put effort into remodeling apartments of tenants he deems undesirable? How does this idea apply to the way principals might deal with mediocre teachers?

3. What happens when teachers punish the entire class for the misbehavior of a few? How do the misbehaving students feel? How do the responsible students feel?

4. What are the repercussions of arguing with a parent?

5. Reflect on the "pay for performance" scenario Whitaker describes. Why does he suggest that the perspectives of the entire faculty were not the decisive factor regarding the program's merit?

Notes

Journal Prompt

The author proposes that we treat everyone as if they were good because we will make those who are good feel affirmed and make all others feel uncomfortable. Consider the graffiti in bathroom stalls that the author mentions. What did this particular school do in an effort to eliminate graffiti? Would such a decision be likely to accomplish the purpose? How will the best students feel about this decision? How will the perpetrators feel? Consider an alternate way of dealing with this student issue in which you treat all students as if they were good.

Group Activities

Dear Parents . . .

On page 98 of the text, the author shares a memo he saw sent home to all parents regarding picking up their children on time. He also includes an alternative letter that is just as effective as a reminder to the parents who are the problem while reinforcing the good behavior of the majority of the parents. In groups of three to five, have participants brainstorm other issues that arise each year, resulting in a letter home to parents (attendance, signing and returning paperwork, students' tardiness, making up work, discipline, sending children with appropriate materials, etc.). Ask each group to choose one topic and write two versions of a letter to parents addressing the issue. The first letter should take the traditional approach, targeting all parents equally. The second letter should be written in the alternative style, attempting to make the parents who act correctly feel comfortable, while making the others feel slightly uncomfortable in the hopes they will change their behavior.

Freeze Frame

Have participants work in pairs and begin role-playing one of the following situations in front of the class. They improvise the scene, but at any moment anyone in the class (including the facilitator) can say "FREEZE." The role-players stop where they are. Then the person who froze the action taps one of the role-players on the shoulder and takes his place in the scene. The new role-player now resumes the scene by talking first, introducing any new dialogue or action she wishes. The new role player can modify the scene slightly, take it in a very different direction, or completely change the topic of the scene. The role players continue to improvise the new scene until someone else from the class says "FREEZE" and steps in to alter the scene once again. This process of improvising, freezing, and altering the scene continues until as many people as desired have taken turns participating in the role-play. In each situation, have principals concentrate on how to correct the undesirable behavior by remembering who is most comfortable and who is least comfortable.

- A small number of parents are dropping off fast-food lunches in the front office to be delivered to children during their lunch time. Children are not allowed to eat these lunches in the cafeteria.
- Teachers are forgetting to take attendance, therefore causing the attendance list to be delayed each day.
- Teachers or students are not following the dress code.
- Students are using inappropriate websites for research.
- Parents are "helping" their children too much with school projects.

Application

Upon returning to your school, examine any student handbooks, parent communications, course outlines, syllabi, and codes of conducts you can locate. Apply the *Who is most comfortable and who is least comfortable in this situation*? standard. Find examples of language that might make your best stakeholders feel uncomfortable while doing little to address those who might truly need to understand the directives and change their behavior. Bring any examples you can find to share at the next class session.

Notes

13

Chapter 16: Understand the High Achievers

Key Concepts

- ★ One of a principal's greatest challenges is working successfully with high-achieving teachers. They do so much for a school that the principal must understand these key people, remain sensitive to their needs, and maximize their ability.
- ★ The very best leaders ignore minor errors. High achievers emotionally deflate when their shortcomings are pointed out by someone else. Faculty members will shy away from and avoid interaction with a principal who harps on minor errors.
- ★ Truly outstanding teachers need two things from principals to make them content and motivated: autonomy and recognition.
- ★ Great principals allow high-achieving teachers to take risks. They do not attempt to control the behavior of less effective faculty members by establishing rules. Every time a rule is put in place, good people follow it and thus lose autonomy. Those for whom it was intended will ignore it anyway.
- ★ Effective leaders consistently acknowledge that what their best teachers do is special and different. Great principals make certain that these superstar teachers know that they are valued and that they make a difference in the lives of students.
- ★ Principals must delegate anything that anyone else can do because there are simply too many things that *only* the principal can do.
- ★ The same rule applies for high-achieving teachers. They should not be asked to do something that another teacher can do. A principal who assigns the best teachers unimportant tasks is wasting a valuable resource. A principal who plans ahead and asks others to take on less essential tasks will protect the high achievers and gain the involvement of other staff members.
- ★ High achievers are among the first to leave a school if they do not feel valued and important. If the principal does not take care of them, someone else will and the school will have squandered its most valuable resource.

Discussion Questions

1. Why is it challenging for principals to work successfully with their highest-achieving teachers?

2. Discuss criticism and praise as they relate to high-achieving teachers. How do superstar teachers react to criticism? To praise?

3. Why is it important to allow the best teachers to take risks?

4. Discuss Whitaker's rule of thumb for principals in terms of delegating responsibility. Do you agree? Why or why not? How does this rule also apply to high-achieving teachers?

5. If a high-achieving teacher and a griping teacher are both unhappy, which is more likely to leave a school? Why? How can principals keep their best teachers? How can principals encourage their less than stellar teachers to look elsewhere?

Notes

Journal Prompt

Whitaker stresses that principals must overlook what he calls "minor errors." Principals vary widely on what they consider a "minor" error. Some are passionate about professional attire and timeliness, while others consider these minor areas of focus. What are some errors you are willing to overlook, particularly as they relate to your high-achieving teachers? How would student success be affected if you completely overlooked these errors? On the other hand, what are a few "nonnegotiables" for you as principal—that is, errors that you feel you cannot overlook? If you are a veteran principal, have your views on this topic changed over time? If you are a new principal, what errors are you willing to overlook?

Group Activities

Evaluating—and Valuing—High Achievers

On page 106 of the book, the author discusses the challenges of evaluating teachers, in particular high-achieving teachers, whose value to the school cannot always be captured in a standard teacher evaluation form. Organize participants into five groups. Have them discuss successes and frustrations they have experienced with various teacher evaluation processes. Distribute one of the following five statements to each of the five groups. Have them examine the assigned statement relating to teacher evaluation in light of high-achieving teachers:

- Place the teacher at the center of evaluation activity.
- Use more than one person to judge teacher quality and performance.
- Use multiple data sources to inform judgments about teachers.
- Spend extensive time and other resources needed to recognize good teaching.
- Use the results of teacher evaluation to encourage professional dossier building.

Ask each group to brainstorm ways of incorporating their statement into their own teacher evaluation practices, particularly for their high achievers. How can each of the above statements be implemented in a way that enhances the professional growth of superstar teachers? Ask each group to share with the large group the statement they analyzed and ideas they came up with.

Getting the Right Teachers

Ask individual participants to list the desired qualities of a high-achieving teacher. Next, have them share these lists with a partner and combine their lists into one streamlined list. Then have groups of four or five create combined, revised group lists. Finally, have the entire group create one final, revised list of qualities. Have new groups of three or four use this final list to create questions and scenarios for interviews to determine whether a teaching candidate possesses the desired qualities of a high-achieving teacher.

Notes

Application

Consider the issue of delegating responsibilities, both for yourself as principal and your high-achieving staff. List your name and the names of any assistant principals and five high-achieving teachers. Try to find at least one duty and/or responsibility assigned to each of these names that, upon reflection, seems less than significant to the core work of your school and that could be delegated to another staff member. List the names of staff members who could assume these responsibilities. Keep in mind that you want your highest-achieving staff members to focus on those things that only they can do. By delegating less significant responsibilities, you free the achievers for more important work and include other staff members at the same time. These activities should not be routine things that everyone takes turns doing (bus duty, recess duty, etc.).

Notes

14

Chapter 17: Make It Cool to Care

Key Concepts

- ★ Effective principals have a strong core of beliefs that guides their decisions and defines their vision for their schools.
- ★ The clearer principals are about their own beliefs, the more effective they can be in working to achieve them.
- ★ The core beliefs can be extremely simple, yet they frame the way principals work in their schools.
- ★ Getting people at the school to do the current thing is fine; getting them to do the right thing is essential.
- ★ Treating people with dignity and respect, having a positive attitude, teaching teachers how to treat students, understanding that it is people, not programs, that make a difference, hiring great teachers, and making decisions based on a school's best people are all ways to cultivate a school environment in which it is cool to care.
- ★ Every principal needs to know which teachers are the legends in the school and work to make sure the ones on the pedestal are the best ones.
- ★ Great principals do the right thing no matter what else is going on.
- ★ Once principals have clearly presented logical reasons for change, resistant teachers will not be swayed by further argument. Principals must understand that behavior and beliefs are tied to emotion and must use the power of emotion to jump-start change.

? Discussion Questions

1. Why is it vital that principals develop core beliefs? What influenced you in adopting your own core beliefs?

2. Discuss your reactions to Whitaker's central core belief: that making it cool to care throughout the school is of paramount importance. Is this a valid core belief for other principals? Explain.

3. Why does Whitaker downplay the importance of getting the faculty to go along with a particular initiative? What is a more significant goal?

4. How can principals ensure that their very best teachers are the ones who are placed upon a pedestal by students, parents, and peers as the school's legendary teachers?

5. Why is it important to consider the emotional side of teachers when implementing change? Discuss ways to deal with teachers resistant to change.

Notes

Journal Prompt

Whitaker shares his own core beliefs in this chapter, most notably that he wanted it to be "cool to care" at his school. On page 112, he describes "The Great Teacher " he identifies as "Mrs. Heart," a staff member who cared about her students and her school and who made it "cool to care" for students in her classroom. In your own words, what is Whitaker's philosophy of education? What was Mrs. Heart's philosophy of education? Do you agree with this philosophy? Take a moment to describe your own philosophy of education, highlighting your simple core beliefs.

Group Activities

I Can See Clearly Now . . .

In this chapter, the author stresses that core beliefs are central to any school's success and he offers his own core belief, his goal of making it "cool to care" at his school. Distribute the following nine statements to each participant. Each of these statements could possibly stand as a core belief of a principal. Ask participants to assign a 1, 2, or 3 to each statement, with "1" indicating a statement that they would fervently support as a core belief, "2" indicating agreement with the statement, but not necessarily a core belief, and "3" indicating a statement that they feel is not significant or that they might even disagree with.

Next, arrange participants into groups of three or four to discuss their individual responses and to arrive at a group consensus for each statement. Post each statement on chart paper on the wall. Ask each group to record their rating of each statement (1, 2, or 3) on the chart paper. Engage the entire group in a discussion of patterns or areas of divergent thinking.

- In our school, we will do whatever it takes to teach, inspire, and motivate all learners, including both student and adult members.
- In our school, we will work collaboratively, focusing on results and learning, sharing strategies that engage learners, and seeking help in areas in which we are struggling to engage them.
- In our school, we will be visible throughout the school. Administrators will be regular and active in their visits to classrooms.
- In our school, there will be no pecking order among our staff members. Those who contribute to the school in advancing our vision will be valued and recognized whether they have one or thirty-one years of experience.
- In our school, we will not give up on our students and we will rely on each other in finding new ways to engage every student.
- In our school, we will not settle for good; instead, we will strive for greatness by continuously exploring new ways of ensuring success for all learners.
- In our school, we will model lifelong learning. All teachers at our school will earn a master's degree. Many will also earn specialists' and doctoral degrees. Many teachers will become certified in the areas of reading, ESOL (English for Speakers of Other Languages), and gifted instruction.
- In our school, we will display teacher and student work throughout the school and beyond. We will recognize and celebrate our successes.
- In our school, we will act on the premise that we are the variables at our school. Superior teaching and leadership are the primary determinants of student and school success. We will not blame outside forces for poor results; we will accept responsibility for all areas of our school's performance.

Tell Me What You See . . .

Have each participant read the passage on the next page, which describes a school in Anywhere, USA. Divide participants into groups of three to five; distribute ten pieces of cardstock paper, each large enough to write a sentence on, to each group. Ask group members to discuss the scenario and surmise the likely core beliefs, vision, and values that are in place and shared at the school. Have each group write at least ten statements that might apply based on the passage. Place one piece of chart paper for each group on the walls of the room. Ask each group to tape their ten statements on a piece of the chart paper and present the core beliefs of the school in Anywhere, USA, as they discerned them, explaining how they arrived at their answers and whether they agree with the beliefs in place at this school.

As you walk into the school in Anywhere, USA, the first thing you notice is the amount of student work displayed on the walls of the school. A number of framed photographs of teachers and students working and celebrating together also adorn the walls. You step into the office and are greeted warmly by the receptionist, who welcomes you to Anywhere and asks if you would like a cup of coffee or some bottled water. She explains that the administrators are not in the office at the moment because they are visiting classrooms, but offers to find a student leader who can give you a tour of the school.

In touring the school with your student guide, you learn a great deal. In the classrooms you visit, you see students actively engaged in learning. Your guide explains that all students are required to complete all assignments. She says that failure is not an option at this school and that if students do not turn work in on time, they will simply have to do it later, perhaps losing a privilege. As you pass one classroom, you notice a teacher other than the classroom teacher sitting in the back, taking notes. Your guide says that this is a teacher from another grade level who must be doing a peer observation. Although students seem to be producing quality work in each room, they also appear to be having fun, laughing, smiling, and interacting with each other and their teachers.

Outside several classrooms, you see adults working with small groups of students. Your guide identifies these as parent volunteers. Your guide introduces you to an assistant principal you meet in the hallway, Mr. Jones. Mr. Jones greets you warmly and introduces several people with him, who turn out to be teachers and administrators from another district who came to observe in the school for the day.

In several rooms you visit, teachers are obviously on planning time, but they are planning with small groups of colleagues, examining student work and sharing strategies for increasing student engagement. In another classroom, a team of teachers is analyzing data from the previous year's standardized testing and establishing goals for the next nine weeks of instruction in terms of standards learned and anticipated performance on common assessments.

In nearly every classroom, you notice two things in common: the standard from the state curriculum being taught and learned is posted at the front of the room and one wall of the classroom is dedicated as a "Word Wall," with vocabulary from each academic discipline posted. As you enter the final classroom on your tour, you observe an educator talking to a class about setting and accomplishing goals. Your guide informs you that this is the principal of the school conducting a "guest" lesson.

Upon your return to the office, you meet a newspaper reporter and photographer who are there to do a feature on one of the teachers, who has been named Teacher of the Year for the entire system. Your student guide shakes your hand and thanks you for visiting the school. The receptionist offers you a colorful brochure describing the school, along with a copy of the most recent monthly newsletter.

Application

On page 114 of the text, Whitaker states that in great schools, teachers tell stories about the teaching legends they have worked with. First, write about one of the teachers at your current school whom you consider "legendary." Then, write about a teacher or principal from your own school days who had a positive impact on you and whom you also consider a legend. Share the first story with the teacher you wrote about by placing it in that teacher's mailbox. Consider sending your second account to your former teacher or principal or to one of their family members.

Notes

15

Chapter 18: Don't Need to Repair—Always Do Repair

Key Concepts

- ★ Effective principals aim to treat people with respect ten days out of ten. They know that a relationship, once damaged, may never be the same.
- ★ Effective principals are acutely sensitive to everything they say and do.
- ★ The best principals work to keep their relationships in good shape, and teachers notice this effort. The principals also work hard to repair any relationships that become damaged.
- ★ Great principals have considerable knowledge of their staff beyond school. They inquire about families, personal lives, and outside interests.
- ★ Principals must work with teachers to build their "people skills." They focus on changing behaviors without necessarily altering beliefs.
- ★ One way principals can repair relationships—and teach their teachers to repair damaged relationships—is by making the simple statement "I am sorry that happened" to parents, students, or others who are upset. This is a powerful defuser.
- ★ In all discipline matters, it is essential that principals focus on prevention, not punishment. A principal cannot do anything about the fact that an incident occurred, but can work to prevent it from happening again.

❓ Discussion Questions

1. Discuss several ways that principals work to establish and maintain healthy professional relationships. Discuss techniques that principals must use in teaching students and teachers how to repair damaged relationships.

2. Why is the simple phrase "I am sorry that happened" such an effective first step in restoring a damaged relationship with a teacher, parent, or student?

3. Why is it important for principals to become familiar with their teachers beyond the school setting?

4. Whitaker states that the critical issue in working to change teacher behaviors is not *why* they change their behavior, but *whether* they change their behavior. Explain this statement.

5. Why is it counterproductive to focus on getting teachers to admit they were wrong? What is a more productive approach?

Notes

Journal Prompt

Imagine (or draw on your own experience) a situation in which parents are visibly upset with you about an incident at school involving their son or daughter (a bad grade, a demeaning comment allegedly made by a teacher about the child, a punishment that the parents consider unjust, etc.). Write about this situation and how it would play out if your immediate response was "I am sorry that happened." Write out a script of responses and follow-up replies in such a situation. Remember: you are not saying the incident was your fault or accepting blame; rather, you are simply starting off by expressing your sorrow that it happened.

Group Activities

Restoring and Repairing

Whitaker advises educators to teach students to behave in a way that "restores" them in the eyes of the offended party. In a traditional approach to discipline, the focus may be on (1) What happened? (2) Who's to blame? and (3) What's the punishment? On the other hand, a restorative approach asks (1) What happened? (2) Who has been affected and how? (3) How can we put it right? and (4) What have we learned so that we can make different choices next time? Prior to class, create four scenarios that might occur in school resulting in someone being adversely affected. For example, a student consistently talks out in class; a student responds disrespectfully to a teacher; a student refuses to complete an assignment; a student uses inappropriate or threatening language toward a classmate. Write each scenario on an index card, and, after organizing the class into four groups, distribute one card to each group. Have each group analyze their assigned scenario and plan out two courses of action, one based on the traditional approach and the other on the restorative approach. Have each group post their two plans on two different pieces of chart paper and present to the large group. Discuss the benefits and disadvantages of the two approaches while focusing on the goals of restoration and repairing.

All the Things We Say and Do . . .

Effective principals are sensitive to everything they say and do. They must have excellent "people skills." Communication involves not only words, but actions as well, including body language. This activity reinforces these understandings.

Before class, copy and cut apart several sets of the twenty-six items on the list below (do *not* include the headings). Provide one set to each group of three to five members. Ask the groups to categorize the items into six groups based on similarities and differences. Do not give any other direction, other than to note that the items all relate in some way to how we communicate—verbally or nonverbally—with others. Allow participants ten to fifteen minutes to sort the items. Have groups share their categories and the discussions that ensued within the groups.

When participants are happy with (or resigned to) the categories they have created and to which they have assigned the items, the facilitator should reveal the actual category headings (eye contact; facial expressions; gestures; posture, body orientation, and proximity; paralinguistics; and humor). These are not distinguished earlier in order to encourage group members to decide on category headings themselves.

Eye contact

- signals interest in others
- increases the speaker's credibility
- conveys interest, concern, warmth
- helps regulate the flow of communication

Facial expression

- provides powerful cues
- often is contagious
- makes person seem warm and approachable
- encourages people to react favorably

Gestures

- failure to use gestures perceived as boring and stiff
- lively and animated gestures capture attention
- perceived as interesting
- head nods indicate listening

Posture, body orientation, and proximity

- stand erect and lean slightly forward
- face each other
- cultural norms dictate a comfortable distance
- improves eye contact
- increases the opportunities for conversation

Paralinguistics

- tone
- rhythm
- volume
- inflection
- avoid speaking in a monotone

Humor

- often overlooked as a teaching tool
- releases stress and tension
- fosters a friendly environment
- must be appropriate

Notes

Application

Take some time in the next few days at your school to focus on communicating with students, parents, and teachers. Ask several students who have attended your school for more than one year to meet with you in your office. Ask them to share something positive about one of their teachers as well as things they wish to see improved in the school, in and out of the classroom. Call five parents at random, asking them what they most appreciate about your school and what they would like to see changed. Ask three trusted teachers how they deal with difficult parents and tense situations with students. Make mental and written notes on the responses of all three stakeholder groups. At the next session, offer to share what you have learned about your school with particular focus on the areas of communication and relationships. Throughout this activity, keep in mind the important issues of sensitivity and confidentiality.

Notes

16

Chapter 19: Deal with Negative or Ineffective Staff Members

Key Concepts

- ★ Dealing with negativity may be the least enjoyable aspect of a principal's job, but it is a critical leadership skill. Allowing negative forces among a faculty to simmer unchecked can eventually bring down even the most positive teachers at the school.
- ★ Every principal recognizes the vast difference between the school's most effective and least productive teachers, and the best principals take responsibility for addressing this gap.
- ★ Great principals recognize that less positive staff members cannot be allowed to obstruct progress toward important school improvement goals.
- ★ Improving the performance of classroom teachers depends on regular classroom visits by school leaders.
- ★ Effective teachers love it when principals visit their classrooms regularly, while less effective teachers would just as soon be left alone. Since principals want their best people to feel comfortable and their less effective people to feel less comfortable, visiting all classrooms regularly is an easy way to accomplish both goals.
- ★ One of the purposes of frequent classroom visits is simply to build a relationship of trust and respect. Another purpose is to visit so often that the principal's presence becomes a natural and normal part of the teaching and learning process.
- ★ Great principals know that their primary obligation is to the students in the school, not the adults. As a result, great principals effectively address negativity among adults in the school, finding ways to change their behavior—or their employment status.

? Discussion Questions

1. Why must principals do something about negative staff members?

2. According to Whitaker, what do the best teachers expect from their colleagues who may not be as effective or energetic as they are? What are the implications for principals?

3. In what ways do adults in schools sometimes behave like children? What must the principal do about this and why?

4. Whitaker emphasizes the importance of principals being visible in classrooms and throughout the school on a regular basis. What are some of the reasons he gives for being so visible? What are some tips he offers about classroom visits?

5. Whitaker states that when he asks principals what they are currently doing to deal with their least effective staff members, a common "strategy" is avoidance. Why do you think this is the case? What does Whitaker suggest about "avoidance as a strategy" and why is it so important that principals act differently?

Notes

Journal Prompt

Whitaker suggests that teachers at any school can be generally classified into categories in terms of their effectiveness as teachers, ranging from "superstars" to "mediocres." Do you agree with this generalization? If not, how would you add to or revise the breakdown of quality among the teachers at your school? He also states that principals who claim they have no weak teachers at their schools are not being fully honest or accurate in their assessment and may simply be avoiding responsibility for doing anything about underperforming teachers. Do you agree with this statement? Why or why not? Assuming you have worked in a school with mediocre teachers, what steps have you taken to improve their performance? Have you ever had to direct teachers to change specific behaviors they exhibited at your school? If so, what was the ultimate result? How do your very best teachers feel about your visiting their classrooms? How do the weakest teachers at your school react? In what ways does this reaction inform how you deal with negative or ineffective staff members?

Group Activities

Changes in Attitudes?

Ineffective teachers cannot be allowed to come to work and feel happy with their job performance. Such a feeling will encourage them to continue operating in the same manner and will discourage the superstar teachers. Principals can use several methods to raise the discomfort level among difficult teachers, yet—as Whitaker points out—simply avoiding the unpleasant situation is clearly not one. Few leaders actually look forward to dealing with the most frustrating, resistant, ineffective, and negative staff members in the school, but all principals should—and the very best ones do. Whitaker indicates that nearly all teachers truly want to do a good job; it is the leader's job to help them reach their goal of doing a good job. At the same time, at almost any school, a very small number of teachers almost seem—based on their behaviors—not to care whether they are doing a good job.

The starting point with truly negative and ineffective teachers is not to focus on their attitudes or beliefs, which are unlikely to change as a result of calm reasoning; rather, principals must focus on their behaviors. Ask participants to think about any teachers at their schools who belong in this latter category, teachers who are extremely negative influences in the school and/or ineffective in their classroom. Refer participants to the following list of traits commonly used to describe such teachers:

- lazy
- unprepared
- negative
- resistant to change
- defensive
- inflexible
- unprofessional
- unorganized
- unable to get along with others
- content-centered vs. student-centered
- absent frequently

Ask the whole group to name additional traits to describe difficult teachers. After compiling a master list (no more than twenty-five), divide participants into several teams and assign an equal number of these characteristics to each team. Ask participants to define specific, concrete behaviors that would cause them to categorize a teacher as "lazy," "negative," and so on. Next, ask participants to focus on the specific change in behavior they would like to see occur. In teams, have members share their experiences holding conversations with difficult teachers in an attempt to change their behavior, including any successes they have had as well as occasions when the teacher in question was unable or unwilling to change.

Finally, ask two members from each team to role-play an occasion when a principal calls in a difficult teacher to discuss concrete changes in behavior that the principal expects to occur. Allow each pair to role-play this scenario for up to five minutes. Afterward, have other group members comment on the approaches that the "principal" took that would work well or suggest how the "principal" could have more effectively addressed the "teacher's" behavior.

Take Five!

Whitaker devotes much of this chapter to the idea that one of the best ways for principals to deal with ineffective and negative teachers is to spend time in classrooms and hallways regularly. Too many school administrators get bogged down with management and operational issues rather than dealing with what is most important in their schools—teaching and learning. Given the multitude of tasks allocated to school principals, it is not surprising that even the most effective and efficient ones find themselves trapped in their offices. Yet to truly serve as the school's instructional leader—and to deal with poor teachers effectively—principals must know how students are learning and how teachers are teaching. There is no way for principals to even know what is going on in the school—let alone improve the school—if they do not visit classrooms regularly.

An added benefit of visiting classrooms regularly is that it is a win-win situation: the very best teachers in the school are glad that the principal visits their classrooms while the least effective teachers are unhappy. If visiting classrooms pleases the best teachers and makes the least effective teachers uncomfortable, clearly principals must make the time to do this. One manageable way to accomplish the goal of visiting classrooms regularly is to "take five," meaning to visit five classrooms every day for five minutes each. Even the busiest school principal can manage to devote twenty-five minutes to classroom visits on most days.

Allow five minutes for each member of the group to respond in writing to the following three questions:

1. Do you agree with Whitaker that nothing that principals do in their office can truly improve the school? Why or why not?
2. Do you believe the "take five" approach to visiting classrooms is a feasible plan for all principals? Why or why not?
3. If a principal followed the "take five" approach to visiting classrooms for the entire school year, would she have a firm grasp on who the most effective teachers in the school are?

Then, ask participants to engage in a "mix-pair-share" activity whereby they circulate silently about the room. When you call, "Time," have them find a partner nearby and discuss the first question, with one person explaining his response and the other partner simply listening, and then responding. Repeat the process for Questions 2 and 3. To bring closure to the activity, challenge each principal and assistant principal in the group to "take five" each school day until the next session, when participants will share their impressions.

Application

In this chapter, Whitaker implores principals to do something about teachers who are chronically negative influences or who are ineffective in the classroom. As a prelude to taking action, he suggests that principals must gain accurate knowledge of who these teachers are and how they affect their students and their colleagues. He devotes several sections in this chapter to what is perhaps the most obvious—and most important—way to attain high levels of awareness: by making frequent classroom visits.

Upon returning to your school, rededicate yourself to making regular, focused classroom observations. Pick a day before the study group meets again when you will visit six classrooms for fifteen minutes each. Determine ahead of time which six classrooms you will visit, intentionally choosing three teachers you consider among the very best in the school and three you consider the least effective or most negative. Focus on three questions in these observations, recording as many impressions as possible: (1) What was the teacher doing? (2) What were students doing? (3) What evidence did you see that the students were learning?

Based on your six observations, reflect upon whether there was a distinct difference between the three superstar teachers' and the three ineffective teachers' classrooms. Continue to focus on these three aspects of teaching and learning as you observe in other classrooms. Next, based on your observations, make a commitment to meet with teachers whose performance is subpar and have honest conversations about what you have observed and your expectations for improvement. Keep in mind Whitaker's admonition that "avoidance is not a strategy." Explain honestly and directly to underperforming teachers what behaviors you expect to see changed. Let them know that you are willing to support them in changing these behaviors—and that you will be monitoring their performance to make sure the behaviors do, in fact, change.

17

Chapter 20: Set Expectations at the Start of the Year

Key Concepts

- ★ One of the most exciting aspects of being a principal is that each day is so different. One of the most challenging aspects of being a principal is that each day is so different!
- ★ The excitement of a new school year provides principals the opportunity to reestablish expectations, introduce changes, and move their faculty forward.
- ★ Principals must help teachers establish classroom expectations for students. The key is to set expectations with great clarity and then establish relationships such that students want to meet these expectations.
- ★ Regarding student misbehavior, effective teachers focus on prevention. Ineffective teachers focus on revenge.
- ★ Principals have a responsibility to support their staff. This is essential. However, unless they shift a teacher's mindset away from revenge, that teacher will never feel supported. Principals must seek different solutions: students who do not repeat their misbehavior.
- ★ Effective principals express clear expectations at the very first faculty meeting of the year. This sets in place an important benchmark that can be revisited if people go astray later in the year.
- ★ Great principals emphasize and establish expectations that express their nonnegotiable core beliefs.
- ★ It is not fair to expect people to adhere to expectations if the principal does not establish them up front. What's more, if the principal has not clearly identified expectations at the start of the year, they may be perceived as his expectations, not the school's expectations.
- ★ Specific expectations may vary from school to school. What is essential is that they are clearly established, focus on the future, and are consistently reinforced.

Discussion Questions

1. Why is it so important that both principals and teachers set clear expectations at the beginning of each school year? How does relationship-building affect the extent to which others adhere to their expectations?

2. Describe the difference between effective and ineffective teachers in terms of classroom management. How can principals make both groups of teachers feel supported in the important area of student behavior?

3. Once a principal establishes clear expectations at the start of the school year, what are some ways that she can reinforce them throughout the school year?

4. According to Whitaker, principals should host a back-to-school night before the first day of school. Explain his rationale and whether you agree.

Journal Prompt

Take a moment to consider what is vitally important to you as a principal in setting expectations for teachers at the outset of each school year. Whitaker shares three of his own expectations for teachers: (1) never use sarcasm, (2) never argue, and (3) never yell. Decide on three expectations of your own. Brainstorm in writing how you can communicate these expectations clearly, how you can ensure that they are consistently reinforced, and how you will react when teachers fail to meet them.

Group Activities

What to Say—On the Very First Day

Have all principals consider the following: The first announcement of the first day of school may be the only day of the year in which you have almost everyone's rapt attention. You have thought through expectations for your own school. Now is the time to present these expectations to your students and teachers for the first time of the new school year. Write out exactly what you will say over the loudspeaker or on camera on that first day of school. Make your announcement interesting, memorable, and concise. Is there a way that you could make your expectations known each and every day? Can you develop a catchy acronym or saying that can be incorporated into posters and other print materials to be distributed throughout the year? How will you make it a part of the everyday culture of your school?

Have all participants read their first-day-of-school announcement to the entire group. Group members will offer positive feedback as well as constructive criticism.

Notes

Application

On page 138 of the text, Whitaker suggests several ways to revisit expectations with teachers throughout the school year, including the idea of incorporating these expectations into a "Friday Focus" memo. Read the following example, written by Jeff Zoul and sent out to his staff on the first Friday of a school year. Think again about your own expectations for teachers and consider writing a similar memo. Try creating your own memo to send out on the first Friday of the new school year.

FRIDAY FOCUS!

> *"Schools are not buildings, curriculums, and machines. Schools are relationships and interactions among people."*
>
> (Johnson & Johnson, 1989)[1]

I hope everyone enjoyed a productive and enjoyable week of preplanning activities. Although Monday will be my 24th "Opening Day," I never lose the nervous edge I felt on my very first day of school when I began my career as a first-grade teacher in Gwinnett County, Georgia. As we begin a new school year Monday, I hope you share my sense of excitement, rejuvenation, and anticipation of what will be a tremendous year of growth for our students and our staff.

As I will suggest on countless occasions during the course of this year, our success as professional educators will depend to some extent on our specific skills and the breadth of our knowledge base. However, I firmly believe that our character and our human relations skills are even more vital to our ultimate success with our students and our entire school community. Nearly every effective educator I have worked with in my career has excelled in the area of interpersonal skills. Although no list of such traits can be thoroughly exhaustive, I do hope that you will peruse those offered below. Let's focus on these human relations skills as we embark upon a noble journey: teaching young people who need and crave our guidance!

- Be willing to admit when you're wrong.
- Be able to laugh (have a good sense of humor) and cry (display empathy and sensitivity).
- Take time to help others.
- Remember how it felt to be a child.
- Be able to resolve conflicts between people.
- Enjoy working with people of all ages.
- Truly care about others.
- Realize that you can't please everyone.
- Be optimistic about people's motives.

1. Johnson, D. W., & Johnson, R. T. (1989). *Cooperation and Competition: Theory and research.* Edina, MN: Interaction Book Company.

Thank you all for your prodigious efforts this week; thank you all for the human relations skills you already possess and practice daily. Let's remember the importance of those listed above as we progress through this year. Remember to set expectations in your own classrooms and then go about building relationships such that your students will want to meet them. I can't wait to see you all in action next week! You hold the keys to success for our students; unlock their hearts and their minds. Have an outstanding week and knock 'em dead (not literally, of course)!

Happy Weekend,

Jeff

18

Chapter 21: Leadership Is Not an Event
Chapter 22: Clarify Your Core

Key Concepts

- ★ The effectiveness of the teacher is the key determinant of the amount of learning that takes place in the classroom. The effectiveness of the principal is the key determinant of the amount of learning that takes place in the school.
- ★ Leaders must know how to indirectly influence the culture and identity of the organization.
- ★ Climate is the tone of the school. It changes from day to day. Culture, however, is almost always the same. To impact the culture, it is often best to start with the climate.
- ★ If we do something today, we change the climate. If we never stop doing it, we change the culture. If we alter something today, we change the climate. If we never revert back, we change the culture.
- ★ There are three components of classroom management: relationships, expectations, and consistency.
- ★ Single events—no matter how fun—do not move and maintain growth in our schools. They can help jumpstart it, but it is up to the leader to provide that consistency that only the best provide.
- ★ The only way to effectively lead a school is to do the right things every day.
- ★ Leaders must work to protect highly effective teachers from mandates that may take them away from or limit their use of practices that they believe in and that have consistently worked for them.
- ★ Great leaders understand culture and more importantly view culture as something they can and should impact. They know that culture is actually a reflection of them and their leadership.
- ★ We need leaders who are sensitive and caring. Our best teachers exhibit vulnerability. They are consistently approachable and sensitive to the needs of others. Leaders have to be this way too.
- ★ Leadership is not an event. It is something you provide your school every day. It takes consistent, effective leadership to improve a school's climate and eventually its culture.
- ★ Every principal has an impact on others. Great principals make a difference.

Discussion Questions

1. Whitaker consistently reminds us that: "It is always leadership." What does he mean by this? Why is it "always leadership"?

2. What is the difference between climate and culture?

3. What are the three components of classroom management? Which is most important in understanding that "leadership is not an event" and why?

4. Whitaker disputes the common notion that leaders must have "thick skin." Do you agree? Why or why not?

5. What does Whitaker mean when he states that, "Culture is leadership and leadership is culture"?

Notes

Journal Prompt

On page 149, Whitaker suggests that great leaders know that culture is a reflection of them and their leadership. Assuming this to be the case, what can principals do, then, to create and maintain a positive and productive school culture?

Group Activities

A Culture Of . . .

With partners or in small groups, take turns sharing three words that describe the culture in which you currently work or have worked in the past. Then, have each individual fill in the blank with five different words: I would like to work in a school characterized by having a Culture of ___________. Have individuals share responses and report out top choices to the whole group. Discuss what intentional actions leaders can take to foster such culture.

I Want That, Too

School cultures are not wholly unlike any organizational cultures; some are better than others. When looking at corporate cultures, the following companies are often noted for their strong organizational culture: Zappos, Adobe, Disney, Southwest Airlines, Warby Parker, Google, and REI, to name a few. With partners/small groups discuss what makes these organizational cultures strong and share any other examples individuals may know. How can our schools create similar cultures? In what ways are school cultures different than these and what things are we unable to do that they might be able to do in terms of creating a solid organizational culture?

Twenty Things

Type each of the "Twenty Things That Matter Most" on a separate slip of paper. Tape each item on a separate desk around the room. Arrange participants into twenty groups (or have them work individually if there are twenty or fewer participants). Start each group at one of the twenty "stations" and have them spend three minutes reflecting on the item at that desk. Have them write examples from the book, or their own experience, that relate to the statement. Have them write why they feel the statement is important.

After three minutes, have each group rotate one desk (moving in numerical order, with those people at desk 20 rotating to desk 1). Repeat the process of reflecting and writing about each statement until each participant or group has moved through all twenty stations. After reviewing the author's core beliefs, ask individuals to think about core beliefs not mentioned in the text that are essential components of their personal mission as a teacher. Allow time for each participant to write two to four additional core beliefs they value as educators. Have each individual pair up with a classmate to share these additions. Encourage individuals to share these with the whole group.

Notes

Application

Consider administering an informal, anonymous culture survey at your school (or complete a survey based on your current feelings about your school). Consider using some or all of the following Likert scale and open-ended questions. What other questions would you add to any school culture survey?

Please rate the following items on the list based on how satisfied are you with the following statements (1 being strongly disagree and 5 being strongly agree).

- Working at our school is a good fit for a person like me.
- The atmosphere at our school is good.
- I personally agree with our school's mission and values.
- We have a positive culture.
- I believe in the work that we do.
- I understand and support our school's mission and vision.
- I like the culture of this school.
- Our culture supports the mission and vision of the school.
- The leaders of the school contribute to the positive culture of the school.
- I have the opportunity to learn new things at our school.
- I have the opportunity to communicate openly at our school.
- Staff members trust school administrators at our school.
- I have the ability to generate new ideas at our school.
- I am able to participate in decision making at our school.
- My relationship with coworkers at our school is positive.

Open ended:

- Do you feel like your work is respected? Why/why not?
- What would make our school a better workplace?
- Do you feel stressed and overwhelmed?
- Do you feel like you can trust school leaders here?
- Do you feel like you have all the support that you need to do your job properly?
- Do you get timely and useful feedback about your work?
- Do you feel like you are being listened to at our school?
- On a scale of 1 to 10, how happy are you at work?
- Would you refer someone to work here?
- On a scale of 1 to 10, how would you rate your work-life balance?
- Hypothetically, if you were to quit tomorrow, what would your reason be?
- Do you feel valued at our school?
- How frequently do you receive recognition from your principal?
- Do you believe the leadership team takes your feedback seriously?
- Do you feel like the school leaders here are transparent?
- With eyes closed, can you recite our school's mission (vision, values)?
- What three words would you use to describe our culture?
- How comfortable do you feel giving upwards feedback to your principal?
- Do you feel like coworkers give each other respect at our school?
- Do you believe we live authentically by our school's mission and values?

- Do school leaders contribute to a positive work culture?
- Do you have fun working at our school?
- We have a culture of (caring, compassion, recognition, feedback, transparency, etc.) at our school.

Notes

Twenty Things That Matter Most

1. Great principals never forget that it is people, not programs, that determine the quality of a school.
2. Great principals have clarity about who they are, what they do, and how others perceive them.
3. Great principals take responsibility for their own performance and for all aspects of their school.
4. Great principals create a positive atmosphere in their schools. They treat every person with respect. In particular, they understand the power of praise,
5. Great principals consistently filter out the negatives that don't matter and share a positive attitude.
6. Great principals deliberately apply a range of strategies to improve teacher performance.
7. Great principals take every opportunity to hire and retain the very best teachers.
8. Great principals employ strategies for recruiting, interviewing, and retaining the best teachers.
9. Great principals understand the dynamics of change.
10. Great teachers keep standardized testing in perspective and focus on the real issue of student learning.
11. Great principals know when to focus on behavior before beliefs.
12. Great principals are loyal to their students, to their teachers, and to the school. They expect loyalty to students and the school to take precedence over loyalty to themselves.
13. Before making any decision or attempting to bring about any change, great principals ask themselves one central question: What will my best teachers think of this?
14. Great principals continually ask themselves who is most comfortable and who is least comfortable with each decision they make. They treat everyone as if they were good.
15. Great principals understand high achievers, are sensitive to their best teachers' needs, and make the most of this valuable resource.
16. Great principals make it cool to care. They understand that behaviors and beliefs are tied to emotion, and they understand the power of emotion to jump-start change.
17. Great principals work hard to keep their relationships in good repair—to avoid personal hurt and to repair any possible damage.
18. Great principals take steps to improve or remove negative and ineffective staff members.
19. Great principals know that leadership is not an event, and that it takes consistent, effective leadership to improve a school's climate and eventually culture.
20. Great principals establish clear expectations at the start of the year and follow them consistently as the year progresses.

Printed in the United States
by Baker & Taylor Publisher Services